The Baby Boy Syndrome
By Aaron Fields

Copyright © 2021 Aaron Fields. All rights reserved.

Published by The Write Perspective, LLC

Dallas, Texas,

All rights reserved. No part of this book shall be reproduced or transmitted in any form or by any means, electronic, mechanical, magnetic, photographic including photocopying, recording or by any information storage and retrieval system, without prior written permission of the publisher. No copyright liability is assumed with respect to the use of the information contained in this book. Even though every precaution has been taken in preparation for this book, the publisher/author assumes no responsibility for errors or omissions. Neither is any liability assumed for any damage that results from the use of the information in this book.

ISBN: 978-1-953962-14-0

CONTENTS

Chapter 1 **Think About Your Decisions**..1

Chapter 2 **Loving Your Mother Vs. Worshiping Your Mother**...................3

Chapter 3 **Prepare Yourself**.. 4

Chapter 4 **Many Layers To The Issue**..5

Chapter 5 **What Is Your Son Supposed To Be?** 6

Chapter 6 **Emotional Abuse**..7

Chapter 7 **What Does Your Son Need?**............................8

Chapter 8 **Consequences of Being a Son Husband**........................10

Chapter 9 **Look At Yourself In The Mirror**..........................12

Chapter 10 **How To Inspire Your Son** ……………………………...14

Chapter 11 **Important Things To Understand**……………………………15

Chapter 12 **Thinking About The Next Generation**………………………16

Chapter 13 **Addressing Our Weakness**…………………………17

Chapter 14 **Contemplate Your Life Before You Have Children** ……………………19

Notes………………………………………………………………………..

Something To Think About Before You Read

"Men are doing the world a disservice when they don't invest in their sons."

----------Aaron Fields

Word From The Author

Society is known for speaking about the deadbeat dad phenomenon and the single mother problem as if they are two separate issues. However, when you think about it, there is only one issue, and that is the man's poor (black man's) decision making. Believe it or not, there is no such thing as a single mother issue. In fact, it is a cultural issue based on the black man's poor decision making and not having the ability to exercise prudence.

From a community standpoint, I am always going to put the onus and the responsibility on the black man because he is the one who needs to exceed expectations. It is his job to understand that the only person he can change is himself. Gentlemen, please understand that you cannot force people to change. Those people are going to either change their behavior for the better, or continue to act in a toxic manner towards you. Either way, it is going to be predicated on how you decide to discipline and conduct yourself.

Black men must understand that seeking love and validation from other people will not work. Therefore, black men must learn how to love themselves and understand that we cannot change anyone else but ourselves. Unfortunately, a lot of black men have trouble understanding this concept because many of them were raised in these toxic and emotional environments, causing them to want to appeal to other people's emotions. In life, you cannot expect other people to show empathy and understand your circumstances. A major reason black men should not expect these other demographics to change is because we are at the bottom of the totem pole.

Disciplining ourselves as men is the only thing we can focus on. We cannot be too concerned with trying to change somebody else's behavior or their perspective. As men, we must make better decisions regarding what we choose to do with our lives and who we choose to impregnate so that way we can avoid unnecessary problems.

Yes, many times when a woman has a child with a man that she no longer favors or respects, she might take out her anger, frustrations, and resentment toward that child. Especially if that child is a boy who just so looks like the father. However, it is also important to recognize that when a man has a child with a woman that he no longer loves and respects, he might develop anger and resentment towards that child. Especially if the child is forming a stronger connection with the mother. Not only this is a major issue, but it is also a manifestation of our weakness and poor decision makings. That is why it's important to take your time with the women you interact with. When you decide to procreate with a woman, make sure that the two of you are on the same page. Especially when it comes to knowing how you want to raise the child. In other words, you can't impregnate a woman just because she has a nice body and a pretty face. When you bring a child into this world that you did not prepare for, your family is going to suffer.

Think About Your Decisions

Although it's important to honor your parents, it is also important for fathers to not provoke their children to anger. Fathers must understand that with great power comes great responsibility to rule justly and with righteousness. In other words, fathers must make the right decisions in their own lives so that their children, especially their sons, can learn from them.

Unfortunately, too many men (young black men) in this society do not have respect for their fathers. Why is that the case? It is because a lot of fathers do not make good decisions. Therefore, this can lead to a toxic rapport between the father and his son and can negatively impact the next generation. That is why it's important to think about the decisions you make. Keep in mind, nobody is perfect and we are all going to make mistakes in life. However, we as men have to develop a much healthier outlook in order to avoid unnecessary circumstances.

The best way to empower someone is through knowledge, wisdom, and instruction. Sadly, a lot of men (young black men) can not think critically because of the coercive environment they were raised in that was not conducive to their overall health and well-being. Even though the black man had a rough upbringing, it is still his responsibility to overcome his obstacles. Eventually, someone is going to have to break the cycle, so it might as well be you.

Please understand that if you have children by a woman in this society and you cannot provide for them monetarily, you are going to be in some trouble. It is the man's job to provide for his children monetarily, emotionally, spiritually, and intellectually. In other words, you must have something to teach your children. That is why it's important to think about the consequences of your actions. When you choose to partake in destructive behavior that is deleterious to you and your community, your family is going to suffer. If you know you are not ready or willing to take on the responsibilities of raising children, do not impregnate or engage in a serious relationship with these women. As a man, you must be prepared mentally, emotionally, financially, and spiritually. If you do not understand the scope of what you are getting yourself into, the results will not end well for you. If you do not have a vision for yourself or do not know what you want to do with your life, people will try to take advantage of you because this world does not care about you. To them, you are just a sexual object, and a financial asset that allows them to get paid off of your poor decision makings and dysfunctional behavior.

Loving Your Mother Vs. Worshiping Your Mother

The mutual inordinate infatuation that both the mother and her son have for each other is preventing the young boy (black boy) from developing a ruling class mentality. It's fair to say that the rapport between the mother and her son is a very strong bond. It's important to understand that the connection between the mother and her son starts in the womb during the prenatal phase. Once the child is born, the connection becomes stronger through breastfeeding and skin to skin, creating a psychological and spiritual connection. Believe it or not, this strong connection also transitions into the social service and educational field. This largely explains why you see a lot of women working at these entities.

It is very important to know the difference between loving your mother and worshipping your mother. Unfortunately, too many men (black men) worship their mothers and because there are not that many positive black male role models in the home, the young black boy cannot develop a ruling class mentality. Therefore, the young black boy does not know how to reinstate himself as the leader. That is why it's unhealthy and inordinate to view women as your master, even if she is your mother.

Although it's important to love and honor your mother, it is not fruitful to view her as your lord and savior. Because many young men grow up in toxic environments without being subjected to healthy male energy, they walk around society trying to fill an empty void. In other words, many of these young men grow up to be angry, confused, depressed and sometimes violent. Keep in mind, a lot of these young men were not fortunate to grow up in a household with a man that knows how to control himself properly and live his life based on specific ordinances. When the father is not present, the child misses out on important life lessons.

Prepare Yourself

You are walking on a dangerous path if you do not understand the difference between loving your mother and worshipping her. If you are not careful, your ignorance can prevent you from establishing healthy relationships with other people. As a man, you must know how to have a healthy rapport with women and if you are constantly worshipping your mother, your mother is going to prevent you from developing a healthy relationship with the women you interact with.

Keep in mind, there is always going to be a tug of war between your woman and your mother. However, in order to be successful, the man must know how to moderate and regulate both relationships. In other words, you as the man have to be the one to preside over both of them. If you allow your woman and your mother to run rampant in the relationship, they will destroy you and the children.

What would be the best way for the man to prepare himself for this relationship dynamic between his mother and his woman? What does he need to do? How should he approach his mother? How should he approach his woman? What does he need to do to keep them from going back and forth and arguing with one another?

_____

_____

_____

_____

_____

_____

Many Layers To The Issue

Now I must warn you, these next few chapters in this book may be controversial and ruffle some feathers. Why is that? Because this book will expose the layers of issues women have experienced in their toxic relationships with unstable men who are groomed to worship their mothers. You have men that are overly attached to their mothers, men with overbearing mothers and men who are not aware of how territorial and dysfunctional their mothers can be.

Unfortunately, there are many mothers out here that have no boundaries and will try to compete with their sons' love interest. Most mothers who act like this rarely have a man or a love life of their own. Although this issue is not exclusive to black mothers, it's pretty common in the black community. Keep in mind, this is not an attack on single mothers (particularly single black mothers who are doing the best they can). Everyone knows that single motherhood is a tough job and believe it or not, there are some single mothers and grandmothers out here who successfully raised well-balanced men.

Another important thing to keep in mind is that some mothers who like to baby and coddle their sons out of habit are not always intentionally being evil and mean-spirited. In most cases, many black households lack strong masculinity and positive black male role models. Because of the lack of strong black men in the community, many women are lonely and struggle to develop a fulfilling life outside of motherhood.

5

What Is Your Son Supposed To Be?

It's important for mothers to understand that your son is not your husband. In fact, your son is supposed to be a provider, protector and leader in the community and in the household. The son is not meant to protect and provide for his mother exclusively. The son is not born to be a replacement for adult companionship. In fact, your son was not born just to keep you company and your son was not created to fulfill the emptiness you have inside yourself.

Do you think it's fair for the mother to view her son as a husband? What are the consequences of the son having the expectations of a boyfriend or a husband? How will this impact his development and relationships with other women? What are some things men in particular can do in the community to prevent the son-husband dynamic from continuing to happen?

_____

_____

_____

_____

_____

_____

_____

_____

Emotional Abuse

Sadly, in many black households, emotional and psychological abuse is being promoted and normalize in the community. One can make the argument that a mother using her son for emotional support in a way that is normal for a boyfriend or a husband is considered abuse and emotional incest. In other words, the mother elevates her son to a romantic status and uses the child as a substitute for an adult relationship.

Believe it or not, treating your son like a husband is a form of abusive parenting because it confuses little boys as it pertains to understanding their role as sons. Mothers must understand that these little boys that they are raising are going to grow up to be potential husbands, fathers and leaders in the community. Mothers, please understand that your sons are not equipped to fulfill your adult emotional needs, and it is not fair to expect little boys to assume the roles and expectations of a husband.

Again, this is not about attacking single mothers or mothers who are not aware of the damage they are causing. In fact, this is a conversation that needs to be addressed more often. It's important to bring awareness to these types of issues, especially if we want to break the cycle. Mothers who treat their sons as husbands are one of the many issues that are destroying the black community. Therefore, it's important for black men to be more involved and proactive in the household and in the community to ease the burden and some of the stressors that a lot of children and mothers go through.

What Does Your Son Need?

Sons need their fathers or a strong positive male role model in their lives. Sons need wisdom and strong masculine guidance. Little black boys need to be around more black men who know how to demonstrate leadership, good decision making, as well as the ability to maintain healthy relationships.

Although sons need their fathers, sons also need their mothers. Particularly mothers that can love their sons and demonstrate healthy feminine expression. It's important for mothers to exude healthy feminine traits so that their sons can learn and understand that women are typically at their best and happiest when they model femininity. However, in order for this to manifest, men (particularly black men) need to do everything they can to not bring any negativity or instability into the woman's life. A major reason most women (black women) don't exude positive feminine traits is because too many men are dysfunctional and spiritless.

As I mentioned earlier, the rapport between the mother and her child is a strong bond that is sacred. So when you have a woman that does not show any love, or compassion, that is a bad sign. Sadly, many parents do not know how to love their children properly. As a result, these children grow up to be confused, angry, and spiritually broken.

What To Tell To Your Son

One of the many things my father has taught me as a child is that life is not always going to go your way. Life is more so about how you respond to certain things when they do not go your way. Please let your sons know they do not have time to quit on themselves and they do not have time to go back and forth with toxic people. If you can provide your sons with help and enough resources that will help them succeed, please bless them.

What are some things you would like to tell your son?

_____

_____

_____

_____

_____

_____

_____

_____

_____

_____

_____

Consequences of Being a Son Husband

Most sons who are raised to be husbands for their mothers grow up to be lost, stunted and confused about adulthood and their role as men. When boys are coddled and pampered, they grow into men who are misguided and emotionally underdeveloped. In addition to that, these young boys also grow up to be bitter and broken. Sometimes, being raised by just your mother can not only stifle your growth but potentially cripple your cognitive reasoning skills, especially when it comes to interacting with a woman and fulfilling the role of a husband.

A lot of young boys grow up seeing their mother carrying the load alone with no help from a man. As a result, many of these young boys grow up into men who expect their significant others and their wives to do the same thing their mothers did. This largely explains why you see a lot of women resentful and exhausted.

When it comes to the realm of men, many women get competitive. Most women compare their life to another woman's life, especially if that woman is being provided for by her husband. Believe it or not, a woman being provided for can create a deep level of jealously and hatred from other women. Strangely, a lot of toxic mothers do not like to see their sons providing for their wives and significant others. These are the type of mothers that will compete and refuse to give up their number one spot with the son. These types of mothers are self-absorbed and too selfish. Therefore, this puts the son in an uncomfortable position of having to choose between his mother and his woman. If a woman is in a relationship with a man that allows his mother to overstep the boundaries, that woman will eventually become frustrated, disappointed, and unsatisfied in the relationship. It is not only important for their sons to leave the nest but it is also the parent's responsibility to raise and prepare their son to be the best man, father and husband possible. If parents choose to ignore this issue, the son will become a liability and another statistic.

9
Look At Yourself In The Mirror

Once again, this is why I keep coming back to the black man, because the onus is on him. Please understand that I love you brothers and I am not trying to attack you guys. I just want you all to understand how important it is for you to be the face of your household and the face of your community. If you want to be a king, you must be the one to preside over your kingdom. Remember, not only a king must always be ready to assume control over any situation, he must also be willing to take the blame when things fall apart.

As soon as you guys start making better decisions and using greater discretions, many of your issues will vanish. As a black man, you cannot keep blaming black women. You know why? It is because most black women will not change. As a black man, you cannot keep blaming the white man. You know why? It is because white men will not change. Are you noticing the pattern? Think about it, why would these other demographics change if they are already in a more advantageous position?

The only person who needs to change is the black man because he is the only ones that has something to gain from changing. These other demographics have nothing to gain from changing because they are above us and have more power. Once black men have a better understanding of how power works, most of them will not get caught up in a lot of nonsense.

One thing the black man must do is start distancing himself from those that are undesirable and toxic. What do I mean by that? To those of you who constantly complain about these low-quality individuals, the best approach is to ignore and minimize your interactions with them. Don't waste your time going back and forth with these individuals; let them self-destruct without getting yourself mixed up with them. Additionally, black men should refrain from impregnating these hazardous and harmful women. A number of women in society may either self-destruct or strive to change for the better, realizing that they need to improve their behavior to be in a relationship with you. However, this can only happen if you, as the black man, set high standards for yourself.

10
How To Inspire Your Son

Brothers, please understand that your son will focus on the things you say and the things you do. One major way on how you can motivate your son is to live out each day trying to become a better version of yourself. In order to inspire your son, it is very important that you, as a man, give yourself a reason to wake up every morning.

Are you good at something? What are your gifts? What do you like to do that gives you a reason to live life to the fullest? Whatever your gift is, please monetize and cultivate it. Please let your son know he will never become whole as a man if he does not learn how to monetize his gifts. Hell, most of you guys are still discovering what your own gifts are. If you like to write, write. If you enjoy painting, paint. Are you are good with your hands? If so, go to a trade school.

Believe it or not, most of you guys have a gift; you just haven't found it yet. Perhaps the reason many of you men have not found your gift yet is because you guys have not been trained to understand what your gifts are and the importance of it. Please understand that if you do not use the gift God has given you, you will not be fulfilled. Why do you think most people in this world are not motivated? Why do you think most people are depressed and not satisfied?

11
Important Things To Understand

It is extremely important for the black man to get his life together. Why is that the case? It is because you have to be healthy and stable in every aspect of your life in order to maintain stability. Trust me, there are some resources out here. All you need to do is apply yourself.

After you get your life together, please understand the type of women you are engaging with. Consider the kind of woman you conceive with and the plan you have for your children. Failing to have a plan for your children will impede their development. The last thing you want is to have chaotic and confused children resenting you because you couldn't make a better life for them.

Unfortunately, most black children, especially black boys, have been set so far back, they become a liability. Many of you black men don't even know your own father. So please do not allow your child to experience the same traumas you faced. Each generation is supposed to get better, not worse. Without guidance, mentorship, or leadership abilities, black men will face major setbacks.

Thinking About the Next Generation

What do you want out of life? What is your purpose? Whatever you decide to do, make sure you do everything you can to improve your life based on the decisions you make. If you decide to have children, make sure you do everything in your power to make their lives better.

What is your life supposed to be about? In life, it is always important to evaluate yourself. The objective for us, as black men, is to build a better life than our predecessors. Some of us had family members who were farmers, sharecroppers, war veterans, and business owners, etc. Now the question is, what are you doing with your life? Are you monetizing the gifts God has given you? Are you living a sovereign life and working towards becoming an entrepreneur?

In each generation, we are supposed to climb higher and higher on the totem pole of society so we can put ourselves and our families in more prominent positions. There's nothing amiss about paving the way for the next generation. There's no logic in engaging in selfish behavior solely for obtaining glory and gratification. It is not beneficial to be idolized and worshipped by those around you.

Addressing Our Weakness

As men (black men), it is imperative that we work on our weaknesses. We cannot be afraid to address and take on issues that are detrimental to the black community. One thing that we as black men need to stop doing is pointing the finger and blaming these other demographics for the issues we are having. We have so many issues in our own community that we do not have time to be overly concerned with what other people are doing.

Unfortunately, many of us are more concerned with maintaining a rivalry with these other groups of people as opposed to focusing on ourselves and monetizing our gifts. Black men must keep in mind that, as a collective, we are not strong enough to go to war with these other demographics. We don't have the ability to strategize and mobilize because most of the males in the black community think and act like women. In order for us to have a chance at winning, we must be strong enough to address and attack our own weaknesses. It doesn't matter how gifted and talented we are. We will never succeed if we don't work on ourselves and confront the inner demons we face.

One of the main weaknesses that the black man has is his over infatuation with his mother and other women. The reason we are at the bottom of the totem pole in society is because we are being dominated by our women intellectually, emotionally and financially, and spiritually. Therefore, society at large doesn't respect the black man. Hopefully, more black men will better understand the importance of becoming a positive influence. In addition to that, black men must make sure they have enough knowledge and wisdom to preside over certain situations before it spills out of control, especially when it comes to child rearing.

It is very important for the black man to have authority over his son. If the black man refuses to love and raise his progeny, the child is going to be led astray. If you don't have a plan for your life and you do not know the type of woman you are impregnating, you are going to set the child back. As black men, we must understand that if we're going to have children, we must love and treat these kids with the utmost importance. As it pertains to our sons, black men must restore that sense of confidence in our young boys. We must teach them how to love themselves and let them know that they're going to become something special in this world.

Contemplate Your Life Before You Have Children

Within the household, most children are accustomed to the woman being the authority figure. As it pertains to the black boy, he is used to listening and following the black woman's lead, which can ultimately impact his relationships with other women negatively. In addition to that, a lot of these men grow up thinking that it is the woman's job to preside over them.

Gentlemen, please understand that none of us are perfect. We are going to face major challenges in our lives. Sometimes we are going to be confused about our life's circumstances and even doubt ourselves. That is why it is extremely important to become healthy and stable in every aspect of your life (mentally, emotionally, physically, financially, & spiritually) before engaging in a serious relationship and having children with a woman.

Always make sure that you're on a pathway that will lead to success and prosperity. What is your vocation? What are you gifted at? In life, you always want to find your niche and monetize it to the best of your ability. In relationships, money will always play a huge role. As a man, if you put a strenuous amount of stress and frustration into the woman's life, she is going to reach a breaking point. Believe it or not, the woman wants you to be a source of knowledge, wisdom, love, and finance in the relationship. There is nothing wrong with women having those expectations for men. At the very least, the man has to have the ability to provide for himself. If the man can't do that, he shouldn't be in a serious relationship with a woman. This is why a lot of women develop anger, bitterness, resentment, and even hatred towards men. Once again, make sure you are striving to become healthy and stable in every aspect of your life before you get into a serious relationship with a woman and have children. There are a lot of older men out here today that regret the decisions they made when they were younger. Please understand that the decisions you make as a man are going to have repercussions for the rest of your life.

Notes

The Effects of Stress on Single Parents

Stress is a major issue in most parents. If left unchecked, it can become detrimental to you overall health and well-being. Keep in mind, it can also have a negative impact on your emotional and physical health.

Physical & Emotional Effects of Stress

- Anxiety
- Depression
- Irritability
- Lack of motivation & creativity
- Lack of productivity and energy
- Decreased immune function and likely hood of sickness.
- Sleep problems
- Mood & appetite changes
- Muscle Tension
- Headaches
- Dizziness
- Digestive & Gastrointestinal issues

Maintain a Positive Outlook

Negative self-talk can have a negative impact on your self-esteem and confidence. As a parent, you should never undermine your mental health and stay away from negative information. If you are not careful, this can potentially spill over into your interaction with your children.

Avoid Negativity

Try to always avoid negativity, even if the negativity is coming from you. In order to stay optimistic and motivated, use positive affirmations to help you.

Build a Strong Support System

There is nothing wrong with building a support system. Reach out to your friends, family members, or even online groups. It's always helpful to have someone to talk to, especially when you need someone to understand the challenges you're going through as a parent.

Don't Overlook your Health Needs

Never overlook your own health needs. Get in the habit of eating well, staying active and get plenty of sleep. Staying consistent with maintaining healthy habits will ensure that you are taking better care of yourself even when things are chaotic.

Healthy Habits & Routines to Practice

- Meditation
- Mindfulness
- Yoga
- Relax Muscles
- Deep Breathing exercises
- Develop positive imagery and visualization.
- Journal writing

What do you plan on doing to lower your stress and not experience burnout?

www.ingramcontent.com/pod-product-compliance
Lightning Source LLC
Chambersburg PA
CBHW081503040426
42446CB00016B/3368